Original title:

Jewel Wisps Under the Unicorn Puff

Author: Linda Leevike

ISBN HARDBACK: 978-1-80563-434-8

ISBN PAPERBACK: 978-1-80564-955-7

Twilight Shimmers Beneath a Glittering Sky

In twilight's grasp, the shadows play,
Whispers weave through the fading day.
Stars begin their gentle embrace,
Painting dreams in the silent space.

Cool winds dance in the twilight glows,
As night unfolds, a secret shows.
Candles flicker in windows bright,
Guiding hearts through the velvety night.

Moonlight bathes the world in peace,
While slumber's song begins to release.
Each star a wish upon the air,
Hope shimmering in moments rare.

Beneath the sky, a tapestry spun,
Magic whispers when day is done.
For every dream that dares to rise,
Twilight shimmers, a wondrous prize.

Celestial Serenades of the Enchanted

In moonlit halls where echoes dwell,
Soft melodies cast a gentle spell.
Notes drift like dew on a summer night,
Embracing hearts in pure delight.

Singing stars in a cosmic dance,
Whispering secrets of fate and chance.
The universe sways to a timeless tune,
While fairies twirl beneath the moon.

Each chord a promise, a hope reborn,
In enchanted realms where dreams are worn.
With every note, the shadows gleam,
Filling the world with wonder's theme.

Celestial beings with voices bright,
Sing of love in the soft twilight.
Through cosmic waves, their songs will flow,
An ethereal gift for us below.

Ethereal Blooms in a Mystical Garden

In gardens where the sunlight weaves,
Bloom petals whisper their quiet leaves.
Colors dance in shades so bold,
Stories hidden, waiting to unfold.

Each flower tells a tale of grace,
Nestled in nature's warm embrace.
Honeyed scents drift on the breeze,
Inviting hearts to rest with ease.

By moonlit ponds where ripples sigh,
Mirrors reflect the deepening sky.
A chorus of crickets serenade,
While night unfolds in lush cascade.

Ethereal blooms, secrets they guard,
In whispers soft, their magic starred.
Fantasy blooms in twilight's fold,
A mystical realm of stories told.

Dreamscapes Adorned with Celestial Light

In dreamscapes vast where visions glide,
Time suspends, and dreams abide.
Celestial light in a tender sweep,
Guides the weary into sleep.

Woven paths of stardust gleam,
Leading souls through the land of dreams.
Moonbeams soft like lullabies sung,
Caress the heart of the young and sprung.

In corners bright, the shadows play,
Casting wonders to drift away.
Infinite skies stretch far and wide,
Holding secrets where dreams reside.

Adorned with light, each moment gleams,
A realm alive with whispered dreams.
As dawn takes flight, the magic fades,
Yet in our hearts, the spark cascades.

Prismatic Dreams in the Realm of Magic

In twilight's embrace, colors gleam,
Whispers of wonders, a children's dream.
Castles in clouds with dragon's flight,
Stars dance above in the velvet night.

Elixirs bubbling in cauldron's heat,
Tales of enchantment in every heartbeat.
With wands in hand, we weave our lore,
In the realm of magic, forevermore.

Secretive fairies in gardens bloom,
Their laughter weaves away all gloom.
Through forests deep, under silver streams,
We chase the echoes of our dreams.

A tapestry woven of stardust bright,
Marbling shadows with shades of light.
The moon, our compass, soars high above,
Guiding our journey through lands we love.

In prismatic hues, enchantments stir,
Crafting the fate we wish to confer.
With each whispered word, our spirits soar,
In this magical realm, forevermore.

Iridescent Glow of Fantasy's Heart

In the cradle of night, where dreams take flight,
A glow emerges, painting the light.
Fairies dance on the edges of time,
Spinning the threads of a mystical rhyme.

Beneath the willows, shadows play,
Where ancient secrets whisper and sway.
In iridescent colors, feelings ignite,
Unfolding the promise of endless delight.

The heart of a dragon, fierce yet kind,
In tales of old, its magic we find.
With words like spells, we write our fate,
In fantasy's heart, where wonders await.

Like ribbons unfurling in twilight's grace,
Each moment a treasure, in this cherished space.
Through labyrinths of wonder, hand in hand,
We traverse the realms of a dreaming land.

At dawn's first blush, the magic is clear,
In each golden note, stories endear.
In the glow of this fantasy, we steer,
Our hopes and dreams forever near.

Fragments of Light Dancing Through Dreams

In slumber's embrace, fragments take flight,
Glinting like stars in the velvety night.
Chasing the shadows that softly weave,
Dreams painted bright, in hues that deceive.

Ethereal footprints on silver streams,
Guiding our thoughts through shimmery beams.
Each flicker a promise, each shimmer a chance,
Inviting our souls to join in the dance.

Luminous touches of laughter and cheer,
Whispers of magic filled with sincere.
In realms uncharted, where wishes convene,
We gather the fragments of visions unseen.

A whirl of colors in patterns spun,
Through twilight's horizon, our journey begun.
With every heartbeat, each tender sigh,
We follow the trails where the dreamers lie.

As dawn's first light breaks the silence profound,
The fragments of night softly scatter around.
But in our hearts' core, they always remain,
Dancing in echoes, a sweet, secret refrain.

Celestial Trails of Mythic Wonders

Upon celestial trails, our spirits glide,
Where echoes of legends and dreams coincide.
Riding the comets that streak through the skies,
Exploring the realms where enchantment lies.

In the murmur of stardust, stories unfold,
Guardians of secrets, both ancient and bold.
A tapestry woven with threads of the night,
Guiding the seekers of miracles bright.

Valleys of twilight, where shadows converse,
In whispers of magic, the realms we traverse.
With hands stretched wide, we gather the stars,
Embracing the magic that always is ours.

Where phoenixes soar and unicorns dash,
In moments of wonder, our spirits clash.
With every heartbeat, we journey afar,
Chasing the glow of each shimmering star.

Through the celestial waltz of the infinite skies,
We find our place where the dreamer lies.
In mythic wonders, our hearts will unite,
As explorers of magic, in realms bathed in light.

Dancing Lights of Dream and Tale

In twilight's glow, the owls take flight,
With whispers soft, they weave the night.
Stars twinkle bright, like stories spun,
In lands where dreams and daylight run.

The fairies dance with gossamer wings,
Each flutter brings the magic sings.
With laughter's grace, they twirl about,
In moonlit glades, they chase their doubts.

A river flows with secrets old,
Its currents hum in tales retold.
Across the banks, the shadows play,
Where night becomes both night and day.

By lantern's glow, the wizards gaze,
At ancient scrolls and endless maze.
With every flicker, thoughts take flight,
In each dark corner, there burns a light.

So drift along with dreams anew,
Embrace the night, let wonder through.
For in this realm where fables weave,
The heart finds hope, and hearts believe.

Radiant Enchantment in the Heart of Night

Beneath the stars, a magic stirs,
With every glance, the cosmos purrs.
A tapestry of twilight hues,
Where secret paths become our muse.

The moonlight spills on silver streams,
As night unravels whispered dreams.
In shadows deep, enchantments bloom,
Unlocking souls from weary gloom.

A chorus sings of love entwined,
In hidden glades where hearts aligned.
With every note, the world takes flight,
In radiant rhythms of the night.

Through forest halls and starlit skies,
The echoes of a thousand sighs.
In soft embrace, the night unfolds,
A tale of warmth, a heart that holds.

So dance with glee, let spirits soar,
In night's embrace, we find the door.
To realms where magic holds its sway,
And dreams ignite the dawn of day.

Mystical Threads of a Woven Sky

In skies adorned with threads of gold,
The tales of ages long unfold.
Each star and cloud, a woven line,
In universe's grand design.

The sun dips low, the canvas breathes,
As glowing hues the evening weaves.
A tapestry of shimmering light,
Where all that's lost finds its delight.

With gentle hands, the breezes play,
They dance through fields at close of day.
Each rustling leaf a story spun,
A whisper soft, a life begun.

The nightingale sings to the moon,
An ancient song, a timeless tune.
In every note, a piece of truth,
United realms, inviting youth.

So look above and let time flow,
In threads of dreams that softly glow.
For in this sky, our hopes unite,
In mystical hues of starlit night.

Dazzling Ambiance of Nature's Kiss

In morning warmth where sunlight plays,
The world awakens, bright arrays.
With every petal, every breeze,
Nature's song stirs hearts with ease.

The mountains rise with majesty,
Standing guard over land and sea.
In valleys deep, the rivers weave,
A melody that won't deceive.

Each whisper of the rustling trees,
Carries tales upon the breeze.
In every footstep on the ground,
The magic of the earth is found.

With twilight's glow, the world ignites,
In dazzling hues, the day invites.
To dance beneath the skies so vast,
And cherish moments that will last.

So let us sit and breathe it in,
The treasures held where dreams begin.
In nature's kiss, we find our bliss,
In every second, every wish.

Dappled Light on Enchanted Wings

In the whispering woods where fairies play,
Dappled sunlight dances on leaves so gay.
Wings of gossamer shimmer in flight,
Chasing the shadows that tease with delight.

Breezes carry secrets from tree to tree,
Ancient tales wrapped in laughter and glee.
With every flutter a story unfolds,
Of magic and wonder, of legends retold.

Through the glades where moonbeams rest,
Creatures of twilight feel truly blessed.
They murmur of dreams that drift on the air,
Carved in the silence of night's gentle care.

Each petal and leaf, a verse in their song,
A spell that resonates, inviting, strong.
In this realm where the impossible sings,
Life bursts forth on enchanted wings.

Incandescent Veils of Fabled Creatures

Where shadows weave tales in the twilight glow,
Incandescent veils of creatures below.
With eyes like lanterns, they peep through trees,
Guardians of magic on soft, whispered knees.

The air is thick with ancient lore,
As secrets unfurl like wings that soar.
Beneath silver beams that kiss the dark,
Fabled companions play, leaving their mark.

In moonlit glades where the wild dreams roam,
They craft a kingdom, their mystical home.
With laughter like chiming of bells in the night,
Each twinkle a promise of wonder in flight.

Veils woven softly with enchantment unfurled,
Tell of adventures in a magical world.
In every encounter, a spark, a new fire,
Incandescent dreams that never expire.

Luminous Secrets Beneath the Moon's Watch

Under the watchful gaze of the moon,
Luminous secrets whispering a tune.
Stars shimmer brightly, a celestial dance,
Inviting the brave to take a chance.

Beneath the night sky where shadows entwine,
All creatures awake, both humble and divine.
Their heartbeats echo in synchrony true,
Sharing their tales in the midnight dew.

Through the veils of dreams, mysteries unfold,
Where courage is measured in stories told.
Each flicker of starlight, a sign from above,
Guides every seeker toward what they love.

With a hush, the night wraps its arms around,
As secrets in darkness are tenderly found.
The moon, a sentinel, watches over all,
As luminous whispers on sweet breezes call.

Glittering Hues in Enchanted Dreams

In twilight's embrace, where colors collide,
Glittering hues in enchanted dreams bide.
Brush strokes of magic paint every heart,
Crafting a canvas where wonders start.

Mist rises softly, cloaked in delight,
A kaleidoscope whispers to the night.
With every breath, a vision takes flight,
Bringing forth creatures that dance in the light.

Under a veil woven from wishes and sighs,
Magic spills forth with illuminating ties.
Textures of stardust and laughter entwined,
Reveal the bright colors that dreams leave behind.

So let your soul wander, let it roam free,
In realms where the impossible can truly be.
Embrace the bright glow of imagination's schemes,
For life is but sparkles in enchanted dreams.

Glistening Visions in a Dreamt Horizon

In the dawn, horizons gleam,
Whispers dance on silver streams.
Clouds like cotton, dreams unfurl,
Echoes sing in a gentle swirl.

Fields of gold and skies so blue,
Magic sparkles, fresh as dew.
Chasing shadows, hearts take flight,
In the day that follows night.

Wonders bloom in fleeting light,
A tapestry of pure delight.
Each soft sigh, a tale retold,
In glistening visions, brave and bold.

Stars align, the world awakes,
With every step, a bond that makes.
Fleeting moments, lost yet near,
In horizons that we hold dear.

Together we weave, fate's grand seam,
Caught in the webs of a daring dream.
A journey onward, hand in hand,
In the heart of this enchanted land.

Fragments of a Myth Under Silver Skies

Underneath these silver skies,
Legends whisper, softly rise.
Ancient tales in twilight's glow,
Fragments shared, the winds do blow.

Mountains echo with forgotten lore,
Ghostly shadows on the shore.
Heroes' hearts entwined with fate,
Sagas spun in realms of late.

The moon beholds each secret grace,
In gentle light, we find our place.
Woven tales of love and strife,
In this tapestry, we find life.

Stars align, a dance divine,
Myths entwined in phantom line.
Every starlit breath a gift,
Through midnight air, our spirits lift.

Wanderers roam in twilight mist,
A treasure found, a moment kissed.
Fragments rise, like echoes free,
Under silver skies, eternity.

Fantasies Woven in Starlight Threads

In a realm where shadows play,
Fantasies bloom at close of day.
Woven tight in starlight's grasp,
Dreams emerge, they softly clasp.

Silver gossamer, secrets spun,
Tales of laughter, love, and fun.
Each bright beacon, a guiding light,
Leading souls through the velvet night.

Whispers linger in the air,
As cosmic wonders lay us bare.
Each heartbeat, a star's embrace,
In this enchanted, timeless space.

Threads of hope and joy combine,
Stitching memories, heart's design.
A world awash in timeless grace,
In starlight's web, we find our place.

Together we dance, bold and free,
Woven dreams, just you and me.
In the twilight, we shall roam,
Fantasies knit, forever home.

Celestial Whirls in the Fabric of Dreams

In the cosmos, colors blend,
Celestial whirls, a timeless trend.
Stars ignite, a vibrant show,
In the fabric where dreams flow.

Galaxies spin, a cosmic song,
In their rhythm, we belong.
With each twirl, our spirits rise,
Captured tight in starlit ties.

Twinkling dust upon our skin,
Whispers beckon, draw us in.
Every breath, a wish takes flight,
In the embrace of endless night.

Through the realms where shadows gleam,
We chase the echoes of our dream.
Moments linger, soft and bright,
Celestial wonders shine their light.

With every dawn, hope's reprise,
Stitched from dreams, a sweet surprise.
Together we wander, lost but found,
In the fabric of dreams, love unbound.

Ethereal Dances Amidst the Fading Light

In twilight's grasp, the shadows play,
Whispers echo where fairies sway.
With every step, the stars align,
In this realm where dreams entwine.

The moon dusts fields with silver sheen,
As gossamer threads weave through the green.
Dancing figures, both bold and bright,
Seek solace in the softening night.

Each twirl and leap a fleeting song,
In the dusk where the lost belong.
With laughter, the night sky ignites,
Ethereal dances, wondrous sights.

Gentle breezes hum ancient tunes,
Inviting magic beneath the moons.
In twilight's hug, the spirits soar,
As the world fades to tales of yore.

Celestial Visions in a Glowing Landscape

In the meadows where dreams unfold,
Celestial visions brave and bold.
Fields aglow with a warm embrace,
Nature's palette, a sacred space.

Crimson skies yield to twilight's kiss,
In this landscape, a moment of bliss.
Luminous orbs dance in delight,
Casting magic in the deepening night.

Stars awaken, their stories shared,
With whispers of hope in the still air.
Each breath we take is a spell released,
Binding our hearts, a timeless feast.

Through the forests where shadows gleam,
We wander lost in a waking dream.
Every rustle and flutterting sound,
Is a reminder of wonders found.

Fantasies Wrought in Twinkling Silks

With threads of starlight, dreams are spun,
Fantasies weave as day is done.
Glimmers and glows in a cloak so fine,
Entwined in whispers, fate's design.

Moonlit tapestries drape the night,
Painting visions in soft twilight.
Where wishes gather and hopes ignite,
Twinkling silks bring dreams to light.

In every fold, a story waits,
In every shimmer, the heart relates.
Beneath the stars, our spirits twine,
In woven tales that are ever thine.

Through realms of magic, let us roam,
In fantastical lands, we find our home.
To dance in silk with every breath,
In dreams alive, we conquer death.

Mystical Hues of a Starlit Symphony

A symphony plays in the starlit skies,
Where mystical hues in silence rise.
Chords of light in a cosmic dance,
Awake our souls with a fleeting glance.

Every note a breeze, every beat a spark,
Illuminating paths in the endless dark.
Colors collide in a radiant flood,
As dreams drift softly on echoes of thud.

In shadows deep, the magic stirs,
Creating beauty in the blur.
Waves of wonder, a cosmic tide,
Carrying secrets where hopes reside.

Beneath the stars, we find our voice,
In melodies born from the heart's choice.
A symphony rich, a starlit lore,
Where the cosmos and dreams forever soar.

Glimmering Secrets in Celestial Veils

In the night sky, secrets weave,
Whispers soft as the autumn leaves.
Stars above in a silent dance,
Guarding dreams as they take their chance.

Moonlight bathes the world in silver,
Each twinkle a forgotten quiver.
Hidden tales of ages past,
In the heavens, magic is cast.

Winds of change through branches flow,
Carrying wishes from below.
Cloaked in shadows, night unfolds,
Revealing mysteries it holds.

Beneath the stars, hearts beat anew,
As the cosmos shares its view.
A tapestry of light and lore,
In celestial veils lies more.

Hope ignites in the quiet space,
As dreams entwine with time and grace.
Glimmers of fate in the night reside,
In starlit paths our hopes confide.

Ethereal Lights of Enchanted Whispers

Beneath the trees, a soft glow gleams,
As twilight weaves its gentle dreams.
Whispers float on the evening air,
Carried by breezes, light as despair.

Flickering fireflies join the tune,
Dancing lightly 'neath the moon.
Each soft murmur tells a tale,
Of magic hidden in the veil.

Veils of mist, ethereal and light,
Wrap the world in a silken night.
Voices of wonder beckon near,
Bringing secrets for hearts that hear.

In the dark, where shadows blend,
A melody that will not end.
Enchanting souls with a tender kiss,
Lost in the ether's gentle bliss.

Ethereal lights shimmer and dance,
In every flicker, a forgotten chance.
Weaving together the night's delight,
In whispers soft, dreams take flight.

Chasing Stardust in Dreamy Meadows

In fields of gold, beneath the glow,
Where secrets of the starlight flow.
Chasing dreams on a zephyr's wing,
In the moon's embrace, hearts take to spring.

Laughter echoes, soft and free,
In meadows rich with symphony.
Sprinkled stardust on the ground,
Every step an enchanting sound.

As twilight paints the world aglow,
Magic stirs beneath the bow.
Here in the stillness, wishes gleam,
Every whisper a tender dream.

Fleeting moments like shadows blend,
Where reality and dreams transcend.
Chasing stardust, we lose the day,
In this meadow, we dance and play.

With every heartbeat, the night reveals,
The wonders locked in starlit seals.
Chasing the echoes of moonlit streams,
In dreamy meadows, we find our dreams.

Luminous Threads in the Misty Glade

In the heart of a whispering glade,
Where shadows linger, softly laid.
Threads of light weave through the trees,
Dancing gently in the evening breeze.

Misty veils hug the emerald floor,
Guarding tales of old folklore.
Each luminous strand tells a story,
Of forgotten paths and bygone glory.

Through the curtain of softest haze,
Lies a world lost in a daze.
Here, the heart finds solace sweet,
As gentle echoes softly greet.

Cloaked in shadows, the spirits play,
Guiding wanderers who lose their way.
With luminous threads, they seek to bind,
The hopes and fears of humankind.

In the mist, where dreams take flight,
Luminous visions grace the night.
Guided by whispers, hearts awake,
In the glade's embrace, we softly shake.

Seraphic Glimmers of Mythical Beasts

In shadows deep, the dragons soar,
With glinting scales that tales implore.
Their fiery breath lights up the night,
While magic weaves in ancient flight.

Beneath the trees, the unicorns roam,
With gentle grace, they call this home.
Their shimmering manes like softest light,
In whispers shared, they take their flight.

The phoenix sings in tones so bright,
A melody to warm the night.
Resurrection in every glow,
From ashes new, they rise and flow.

Through hidden paths where fairies tread,
With laughter sweet, their whispers spread.
They dance on beams of moonlit dreams,
In seraphic glimmers, joy redeems.

When twilight falls, the beasts unite,
In harmony beneath the light.
The world awakens, magic streams,
As myth and wonder weave our dreams.

Twinkling Echoes in a Twilight Paradise

In twilight's glow, the stars appear,
Whispers soft, the night draws near.
Each twinkle spun from dreams revealed,
In twilight's arms, our hearts are healed.

Beneath the veil of violet skies,
We chase the echoes, our spirits rise.
With every breath, the magic sighs,
In paradise where wonder lies.

The moonlight bathes the world in song,
Creating tales where we belong.
With every flicker, shadows play,
As night becomes a soft ballet.

The constellations tell their tales,
Of ancient quests and fleeting trails.
In secret glades, we find our way,
Among the dreams that softly sway.

As darkness wraps the faded day,
Our hopes and fears begin to sway.
With twinkling echoes, spirits dance,
In twilight's glow, we find our chance.

Unicorn Dreams in a Shimmering Dance

In moonlit glades where wonders gleam,
The unicorns dance in twilight's beam.
With hooves of silver on emerald grass,
They prance through dreams, let time surpass.

Their eyes reflect the stars above,
Each glance a whisper, pulse of love.
In shimmering coats of purest white,
They weave enchantments through the night.

With each soft step, a breeze is born,
The air alive, with magic worn.
In circles twirling, they twine and play,
A dance of joy at end of day.

Beneath the arch of starlit skies,
They cast sweet spells and joyful sighs.
In unity, the night they grace,
With every move, a soft embrace.

So close your eyes to dreams anew,
And find the magic waiting for you.
In unicorn dreams, let spirits soar,
In shimmering dance, forevermore.

Radiant Hues of Fantastical Flights

From heights unseen, the griffins dive,
With wings aflame, they come alive.
In radiant hues, the heavens call,
With every beat, the world enthralls.

Through azure skies, their shadows play,
In fantasy where dreams hold sway.
With piercing cries, they chase the light,
In vibrant arcs of endless flight.

The skies aflutter with colors bright,
A canvas painted in sheer delight.
With every swirl, a whisper flows,
In fantastical flights, the wonder grows.

And when the sun dips low with grace,
The night unfolds, a soft embrace.
Stars emerge like fireflies bright,
Guiding the dreams through endless night.

In twilight's grasp, we hear their call,
As magic reigns and shadows fall.
In radiant hues, let spirits glide,
Through fantastical flights, our dreams abide.

Floating Glimmers in the Realm of Hope

In soft whispers of dawn's embrace,
Dreams awaken with gentle grace.
They dance on the edge of a new day,
Casting shadows of worry away.

With hearts bright as the morning sun,
Every journey has just begun.
Faint glimmers that twinkle and sway,
They promise light in the darkest fray.

Amongst the clouds that gently float,
Each thought a feather, each hope a boat.
Sailing on winds of what might be,
Too free to bind, too wild to see.

In the realm where wishes are spun,
Every battle fought is never done.
Yet courage fuels our weary souls,
As hope unfurls and brightly rolls.

So cherish the moments filled with light,
For secrets linger in the night.
In glimmers small, our hearts will cope,
And weave a tapestry of hope.

Sparkling Shades in a Magical Tapestry

In the air, where magic swirls,
Colors dance and secrets twirl.
Threads of light weave tales untold,
In dazzling shades of scarlet and gold.

Flashes of laughter through leaves and skies,
Echo of whispers where enchantment lies.
The tapestry of dreams, alive and bright,
Reflecting all that captures the light.

Every hue holds a story profound,
In each stitch, wisdom is found.
Crimson and azure, they blend and play,
Creating a symphony in bright array.

Among the shadows, shadows shift,
A realm where every heart can lift.
The art of magic in every seam,
An endless world, alive with dream.

So wander through this vibrant thread,
Where every hope and wish is fed.
In sparkling shades, we find our way,
A magical dance where dreams will stay.

Glistening Petals of Mystical Stories

Beneath the moon's soft silvery glow,
Petals whisper secrets only they know.
In grooves of time, where legends reside,
Mystical stories in petals abide.

Each bloom unfolds a tale revered,
Of valiant hearts and hopes persevered.
In colors bright, they shimmer and sway,
Inviting dreams to join the ballet.

Crimson splendor and violet hue,
Paint the pathways with tales anew.
In gardens where magic interplays,
Glistening petals brighten our days.

With every dawn, they greet the sun,
In every petal, a battle won.
Resilience rests in their soft embrace,
A testament bright to nature's grace.

So listen closely to the blooms around,
For in their language, wisdom is found.
Glistening petals share stories' bliss,
Creating echoes we must not miss.

Enchanted Glimmers Beneath a Starlit Sky

Under stars, where magic is spun,
Whispers flutter, and dreams have begun.
The night is alive with wishes alight,
Carried on winds that dance in the night.

Glistening glimmers across the vast sea,
Moments of wonder fill hearts that are free.
In the velvet dome, secrets are told,
Of journeys bright and destinies bold.

Each twinkle shines with a promise clear,
A guide for the lost, a companion near.
In shadows deep, the stars gently play,
Reminding us love will light the way.

As moonlight bathes the world in grace,
Dreams entwine in a soft embrace.
In quiet stillness, they gather and rise,
Enchanted glimmers under starlit skies.

So let your spirit soar, take flight,
Follow the glimmers through the night.
For beneath the stars, all dreams align,
In endless wonder, hearts intertwine.

Ethereal Heartbeats of a Dreamer's Sky

In whispers soft, the starlight gleams,
Awakening the weight of dreams.
A canvas vast, where shadows dance,
In twilight's hold, we take a chance.

With every pulse, the cosmos hums,
A symphony where magic comes.
The silver threads of fate entwine,
In the silent night, the stars align.

Winds of hope caress our cheeks,
As we embark on journeys sleek.
Each heartbeat feels like fleeting time,
A rhythm sweet, a whispered rhyme.

Through eye of night, the spirits soar,
To realms where heart and sky are lore.
Embrace the tides of endless space,
Where dreams will sparkle, dreams will grace.

So close your eyes and drift away,
To where the skies are made of play.
In ethereal realm, our hearts will see,
The endless song of destiny.

Beaming Lights Through the Forest Grove

In emerald shades, the sunlight breaks,
Through tangled limbs, the forest wakes.
Each beam a note in nature's song,
Where echoes call, and hearts belong.

The path winds softly, shadows creep,
Through ancient woods where secrets sleep.
With every step, a story weaves,
Of whispered dreams and rustling leaves.

A gentle breeze, a fleeting chill,
The forest breathes, alive, in thrill.
Among the ferns, the wonders gleam,
And every corner hides a dream.

Where foxes dance and fairies twirl,
In spells of light, the branches swirl.
The heart ignites, with wild delight,
In nature's clutch, the world feels right.

So take my hand, together we'll roam,
Through beaming lights, we'll find our home.
In whispers light, our spirits thrive,
In forest groves, our hearts alive.

Resplendent Fragments of a Dreamer's Heart

In shadows deep, the heart does pulse,
A rhythm born from chance and lulls.
Each fragment glows with hopes untold,
A tapestry of dreams, unfold.

Like jeweled stars against the night,
In every tear, a flash of light.
For in the depths of longing's call,
Resplendent fragments rise and fall.

With every wish upon a star,
We chase the echoes, near and far.
In whispered winds, our secrets blend,
As every heartbeat finds a friend.

Through trials faced, our courage gleans,
In darkest hours, we find our means.
Together, stitched by fates' own thread,
In dreamer's heart, our journey's led.

So raise your voice, let echoes start,
For we'll shine bright, with every spark.
In beautiful chaos, we entwine,
Resplendent fragments, dreams align.

Magical Luminescence in a Twilight Realm

In twilight's cloak, the magic stirs,
As silver glows, and darkness purrs.
A waltz of shadows, sweetly spun,
As day departs, and night is won.

With starlit whispers, softly shared,
In realms of dreams, the heart is bared.
Each glimmer soft, a tale untold,
In magical hues, the world unfolds.

From fireflies' dance to moonlit streams,
In every moment, the spirit beams.
The twilight hums a crystal song,
Where all our hearts are known and strong.

Through enchanted dusk, we wander wide,
In every smile, our fates collide.
In gentle light, we weave our fate,
In twilight realms, we elevate.

So close your eyes and breathe it in,
The magic flows from deep within.
In luminescence, love defines,
A twilight realm where hope aligns.

Radiant Threads in Twilight's Embrace

In twilight's warm and gentle glow,
Where shadows stretch and whispers flow,
A tapestry of dreams unfolds,
In colors rich and stories told.

The stars ignite with silver lace,
Each twinkle holds a secret place,
Where hearts entwined in silent glee,
Compose a song of mystery.

The moon, a lantern in the night,
Guides wandering souls with soft, pale light,
Beneath its gaze, the world awakes,
As dawn approaches, stillness breaks.

With every thread, a tale is spun,
Of battles lost and victories won,
Through every fiber, magic weaves,
A promise held beneath the leaves.

So let us wander hand in hand,
Through twilight's realm, a dreamland grand,
Where radiant threads of hope remain,
Entwined forever in love's refrain.

Gossamer Mysteries of Starlit Meadows

In meadows soft where shadows sigh,
And twinkling stars adorn the sky,
Gossamer threads of silver light,
Weave stories whispered through the night.

With each cool breeze, a secret stirs,
A dance of dreams through tiny furs,
Where fireflies flicker, wild and free,
In this enchanted tapestry.

The moonlit path, a glowing seam,
Leads us along, where wishes gleam,
And every heartbeat echoes clear,
The magic of the night draws near.

Beneath the branches, shadows play,
Their laughter rings through night and day,
As whispers lift on wings of fate,
In hushed reverence, we await.

So step with me in twilight's glow,
And let the mysteries gently flow,
For in this realm of dreams and truth,
Gossamer threads of joy bear youth.

Chasing Rainbows Through Shimmering Fields

In fields adorned with colors bright,
We chase the rainbows in their flight,
Each hue a promise, bold and clear,
That whispers dreams for all to hear.

The dewdrops glisten, fresh as dawn,
A symphony of light is born,
As nature sings a vibrant tune,
Beneath the watchful eye of moon.

With every step, the earth awakes,
As laughter dances, joy remakes,
The warmth of sun upon our skin,
Invites the magic to begin.

Through shimmering paths where wishes flow,
And gentle winds, like secrets, blow,
We trace the arcs of dreams untold,
In every shade, a story bold.

So let us run where colors blend,
A journey endless without end,
For in the heart of every field,
Are dreams alive, and joy revealed.

Ethereal Dances of Mythical Souls

In twilight's hush, where shadows play,
Ethereal souls find their way,
They twirl and spin in moonlight's gleam,
A dance of whispers, a waking dream.

With laughter bright, they swirl around,
In symphonies of forgotten sound,
Where every note, a story shares,
Of ancient times and whispered prayers.

The stars above, a watchful host,
Bear witness to what we cherish most,
A tapestry of time unfurls,
As magic weaves through distant worlds.

In every heartbeat, legends drift,
As spectral beings in shadows lift,
They beckon forth those with the heart,
To join their waltz in realms apart.

And so we sway, in soft embrace,
Lost in the charm of this hallowed space,
For in each dance, a truth unfolds,
Of mythical tales and love retold.

Ephemeral Lights in a Star-kissed Night

In the depths of a night so fine,
Stars twinkle bright, a jewel line.
Whispers of magic fill the air,
Glimmers of dreams beyond compare.

The moonlight dances on silver streams,
Illuminating the world of dreams.
Each flicker tells a tale untold,
Of adventures waiting to unfold.

Crickets sing a tune of delight,
Echoing soft in the warm twilight.
A breeze carries secrets, sweet and light,
Underneath the stars, an enchanting sight.

Shadows may linger, soft like a sigh,
Yet in their midst, the wonders lie.
For every shadow has its own spark,
Guiding lost hearts through the dark.

A night like this, a fleeting dream,
Where light and dark blend in a beam.
Hold close this magic, so rare and bright,
For tomorrow shall chase away the night.

Enchanted Shadows of the Whispering Woods

In woods where thickets whisper low,
Shadows dance, and secrets flow.
Beneath the leaves, old tales reside,
In every creak, the magic bides.

Moonlit paths, where spirits drift,
Through tangled vines, the world's a gift.
In silence, stories come alive,
Where the very shadows seem to thrive.

Mossy carpets cushion the ground,
Where ancient whispers can be found.
Each rustling leaf, a fleeting thought,
A tale of wonders, sweetly wrought.

Flickering lights, like fireflies play,
Guiding lost souls who've lost their way.
In the heart of the woods, mysteries loom,
Waiting for hearts that dare to presume.

So wander far through twilight's breath,
Embrace the thrill, defy all depth.
For in the shadows, magic sways,
And the whispering woods sing of brighter days.

Dreamy Hues of a Forgotten Realm

In realms where colors softly blend,
Dreamy hues, the heart's true friend.
Every shade, a tale to weave,
A tapestry of what we believe.

Glimmers of gold and azure skies,
Dance upon where memory lies.
Crimson petals and emerald trees,
Whisper of magic on a gentle breeze.

Fleeting moments caught in time,
Echo in verses, a child's rhyme.
Where the sun meets the river's glance,
Dreams awaken, begin to dance.

Through twilight whispers, shadows swell,
In the quiet, there's so much to tell.
A forgotten realm, a safe retreat,
Where heart and soul will always meet.

So paint your visions across the air,
With each stroke, a world laid bare.
In dreamy hues, let your spirit roam,
In the embrace of a place called home.

Silvery Threads of Ethereal Whimsy

In the world of dreams where fairies play,
Silvery threads weave night and day.
Glimmers of laughter, soft and true,
A fabric stitched from hopes anew.

Twinkling lights in a twilight glow,
Guide the lost where wildflowers grow.
Each step taken, a magical rhyme,
Entwined with echoes of cherished time.

Whimsy dances in every glance,
As stardust weaves its curious dance.
In the heart of the night, a story is spun,
Of adventures waiting for everyone.

Through the mist, enchanted dreams fly,
On wings of wonder that brush the sky.
Each silken thread a wish unfurled,
Binding the magic in this world.

So wrap yourself in the splendor bright,
Let your spirit soar, take flight.
For in ethereal whimsy we find,
The threads of magic that bind mankind.

Shimmering Dreams of an Ancient Lore

In twilight's glow, where secrets lie,
A tapestry woven in the night sky.
Stars twinkle softly, a guiding flame,
Whispers of magic, calling my name.

Through shadowed paths, old tales unfold,
Of heroes and spirits, of treasures untold.
Elixirs of dreams in the moonlight's grace,
Embodying echoes of a forgotten place.

With every heartbeat, the cosmos sighs,
Awakening wonders that never truly die.
In shimmering shades, both bright and rare,
The threads of time bind the heart's quiet prayer.

The ancient woods cradle stories deep,
In silence they stir, as the night winds sweep.
A dance of shadows, a flickering flame,
Illuminates paths where the brave stake their claim.

As dawn approaches, dreams slip away,
Yet echoes of magic in the light will stay.
For each shimmering star is a hope we hold,
A promise of adventure, forever bold.

Beyond the Veil of Enchanted Night

Beyond the veil where the wild things dwell,
In gardens of mystery, cast a spell.
Moonlit blossoms sway in a breathless trance,
Inviting the dreamers to join in the dance.

Whispers of fairies flit through the air,
Stirring the leaves, with a flicker of flair.
Their laughter entwines with the silken breeze,
As shadows collapse beneath ancient trees.

Here lies the realm where the starlight weaves,
A tapestry brilliant that beckons and leaves.
In corners of wonder, where shadows play,
Dancing with spirits until break of day.

Moments hang heavy like dew on a rose,
Fleeting as twilight before daylight shows.
Yet in this embrace of the midnight's glow,
Lies the magic that only the heart can know.

So linger a while, in this tranquil space,
Let your thoughts soar free, find your own grace.
In the tapestry woven of dreams and delight,
Find your true self—beyond the veil of night.

Prismatic Whispers Beneath Ancient Trees

Beneath ancient trees where the whispers are real,
Colors of magic begin to congeal.
A symphony hums in the rustling leaves,
Each note carries stories that time gently weaves.

Sunbeams descend in a dance of delight,
Illuminating shadows that shimmer with light.
In the tapestry threaded with nature's embrace,
Life's vibrant pulse quickens in this sacred space.

Where dreams take flight on the wings of a breeze,
The heart's deepest longings flow free among trees.
With every step forward, a promise unfolds,
Of mysteries waiting in the heart's hidden folds.

The rustle of secrets escapes through the air,
Echoing softly, a gentle affair.
In each shifting shadow, a vision takes form,
Cradling the whispers that beckon the warm.

So listen intently beneath branches wide,
For every soft murmur and shifting tide.
In the intersection of light and decree,
Lie prismatic whispers just waiting for thee.

Celestial Glints in the Garden of Night

In the garden of night where dreams are reined,
Celestial glints dance, though seldom retained.
With stardust sprinkled upon every flower,
The cosmos awakens, revealing its power.

Moonlight drapes softly over the shrouded land,
Guiding the lost with a gentle hand.
In each fragrant petal, a story is spun,
Of love everlasting and battles hard-won.

Through shadows that pirouette in the dark,
A symphony rises; the night holds a spark.
The whisper of secrets in rustling leaves,
Carries the charm that the heart believes.

Wander these pathways of silver and gold,
Where time is but fleeting and dreams can unfold.
For in this embrace lies a mystery's might,
Awakening visions in the garden of night.

So delve into depths where the ethereal glows,
Discover the wonders that nature bestows.
In celestial dances, enchantment ignites,
A journey of magic in the garden of night.

Shades of Light in Myth's Embrace

Beneath the trees where shadows play,
A tale unfolds at close of day.
Golden beams entwine with night,
Dancing softly, pure delight.

Fables born in twilight's glow,
Whisper secrets, long ago.
In every leaf, a story weaves,
Crafted gently by the eves.

Colors shift as stars appear,
Magic lingers, drawing near.
With every rustle, dreams ignite,
In these shades, both dark and bright.

Mysterious forms start to roam,
Within the woodland, find a home.
Faint echoes of lost refrain,
In myth's embrace, none are in vain.

Through shadows deep, the heart shall soar,
In the quiet, evermore.
Chasing glimmers, shadows fade,
In this realm, where hopes are laid.

Ethereal Beauty in the Canopy Above

In the forest, where dreams align,
Branches twist, and stars entwine.
Emerald whispers in the air,
A beauty found, beyond compare.

Sunlight dances through the leaves,
Rustling softly, nature weaves.
Each petal kissed by morning's grace,
Wonders bloom in this sacred space.

A chorus sings, a symphony,
Of creatures small, both wild and free.
In this haven, hearts are light,
Every moment pure delight.

As twilight paints the sky in hue,
Shadows stretch, the day bids adieu.
Stars awaken, people dream,
In this canopy, magic's theme.

To wander under starlit skies,
Is to glimpse where beauty lies.
Each leaf a page, each branch a rhyme,
In the forest's song, we find the time.

Whispering Petals in Twilight's Hold

In gardens strewn with softest light,
Petals whisper, shy and bright.
Veils of color, gentle sighs,
In twilight's hold, their beauty lies.

Cascading blooms like dreams set free,
Flutter softly on the breeze.
Each a wish, a hope, a prayer,
In the stillness, all laid bare.

Through fields that shimmer, time stands still,
Magic lingers, hearts to fill.
Dusk embraces, shadows sway,
As daylight gently fades away.

Stars awaken in their hush,
In the night, the petals blush.
Underneath the moon's soft beam,
Every flower holds a dream.

In whispers soft, tales are spun,
Of love once lost, and battles won.
A tapestry of night unfolds,
In twilight's hold, a truth retold.

Shimmering Fantasies in a Whispered Breeze

Through meadows vast, where wildflowers sway,
Shimmering fantasies come out to play.
Every petal kissed by the sun,
In laughter, life has just begun.

Breezes carry the scent of dreams,
In nature's arms, the world redeems.
With twinkling stars, the night ascends,
In whispered tales, where magic bends.

Life's a dance on the edge of night,
Each heartbeat echoes pure delight.
In every gust, a secret sings,
Of hidden paths and wondrous things.

Like silver threads in the moonlit air,
Glimmers of hope, each soul laid bare.
From distant realms, soft echoes rise,
Transported dreams beneath the skies.

In every rustle, whispers weave,
Of legends lived, of hearts that believe.
In shimmering light, we find our place,
In whispered breezes, dreams embrace.

Resplendent Echoes of Nature's Embrace

In the heart of the forest, shadows play,
Leaves dance gently, in the light of day.
Whispers of magic float in the air,
Every step taken, a secret to share.

Mountains stand tall, draped in a mist,
Nature's embrace, a comforting kiss.
Rivers sing softly, their stories unfold,
In resplendent echoes, a beauty untold.

Flowers awaken, their colors ablaze,
Painting the landscape in vibrant arrays.
Gentle creatures, both shy and bold,
In nature's embrace, their tales are retold.

A symphony rises, a chorus of glee,
The heartbeat of earth, a song wild and free.
Stars weave their wishes, in twilight's soft glow,
Resplendent echoes, where wonders bestow.

With every sunrise, new dreams take flight,
Nature cradles them, wrapped in pure light.
Hand in hand, we dance in this space,
In resplendent echoes of nature's embrace.

Whispers of Radiant Wishes in the Dawn

In the morning light, dreams take their course,
Wishes unfold from a gentle source.
Radiant blooms greet the sun's golden ray,
Whispers of hope usher in the day.

A dove coos softly, a promise begins,
The world awakens, shedding its sins.
Mountains eye the horizon, steadfast and tall,
Wishes like petals, each one a call.

Upon the breeze, laughter does weave,
Stories of hearts that dare to believe.
Sunlight cascades, painting skies bright,
Whispers of wishes take glorious flight.

Morning unfurls, with its palette divine,
Every moment savored like sweet, aged wine.
Golden horizons, where dreams intertwine,
Whispers of wishes in the dawn brightly shine.

As shadows recede, opportunities dance,
Life's melody plays, beckons a chance.
With every sunrise, a new song is drawn,
Whispers of radiant wishes in the dawn.

Enchanted Glimmers Dancing on the Breeze

In the twilight hour, magic takes hold,
Glimmers of dreams, both tender and bold.
Dancing on breezes, like fireflies' flight,
Whispers of wonder craft stories at night.

Moonbeams cascade, silver and sleek,
Painting the world in a hush, soft and meek.
Each rustle of leaves, secrets are spun,
Enchanted glimmers, where shadows run.

Crickets sing softly, their lullabies clear,
Nature's sweet chorus, drawing you near.
Stars in the heavens, a shimmering tease,
Enchanted connections, dancing on the breeze.

The night holds its breath, time melts away,
Magic unfolds in a whimsical play.
With each beating heart, the universe sways,
Enchanted glimmers in luminous displays.

So hold tightly your dreams as the night whispers low,
In the realm of the stars, let your spirit glow.
For life is a dance, in the shadows and trees,
Enchanted glimmers, in rhythm with the breeze.

Sparkling Stars within a Whispered Tale

Beneath a vast canvas, stars brightly gleam,
Kisses of light, weaving a dream.
Whispers of legends, twinkling afar,
Sparkling secrets within every star.

Stories unfold with a gentle sigh,
Mysteries linger in the calm night sky.
Every flicker and spark, a tale to be spun,
Echoes of worlds where the light has run.

With wishes unfurling, like petals in bloom,
Galaxies whisper from the evening's gloom.
Hearts come alive, intertwined with fate,
Sparkling stars, guiding dreams that await.

A tapestry woven with threads of pure light,
Each star a beacon through the velvety night.
Let your spirit soar, let your heart sail,
For magic is found in this whispered tale.

So close your eyes tight and drift far away,
In the arms of the cosmos, let your thoughts play.
For the universe beams with a soft, knowing trail,
Sparkling stars within a whispered tale.

Enigmatic Gleams of Ethereal Creatures

In the hush of twilight's grasp,
Shadows dance with a silken clasp,
Whispers weave through ancient trees,
Mysteries carried on the breeze.

Glimmers form in twilight glow,
Fleeting glimpses, soft and slow,
Creatures spun of light and mist,
In the dark, can you resist?

Fae reflections shimmer bright,
Guiding dreams through endless night,
With laughter bright as moonlit streams,
They lead us into wild dreams.

Glistening wings in emerald flights,
A chorus sings of starry nights,
Through tangled roots and blossoms wide,
The magic calls us deep inside.

As dawn approaches, secrets glow,
Revealing spells that ebb and flow,
In whispers soft, the world awakes,
Ethereal love, the heart now aches.

Luminous Fantasies in the Realm of Dreams

In the depths of slumber's grasp,
Wondrous forms within us clasp,
Colors shift and shadows play,
Dreams unfold in bright array.

A tapestry of whispers rare,
We travel realms beyond compare,
Where wishes dance on silver strands,
And hope alights in gentle hands.

Crimson skies and sapphire streams,
We sail through worlds adorned with dreams,
Each heartbeat drifts on starlit waves,
In this realm, the spirit braves.

The moon will guide our wandering gaze,
Through twilight's maze, our hearts ablaze,
With every sigh, a magic breath,
Enchanting tales of life and death.

As dawn approaches, dreams retreat,
Yet linger still in heartbeats sweet,
A promise forged in night's embrace,
A luminous dance, time's gentle grace.

Whispered Colors in the Breeze of Dawn

In morning's glow where silence sways,
Colors bloom through golden rays,
Whispers sail on dawn's soft sigh,
Painting dreams across the sky.

Petals scatter through the air,
Carried lightly, scents so rare,
A symphony of nature's song,
Awakens life where we belong.

Dewdrops glisten, jewels of light,
As daybreak dances, spirits bright,
Across the fields where shadows play,
Hope arises with the day.

Every breeze a gentle kiss,
Filling hearts with tender bliss,
In the tapestry of morn's embrace,
We find our dreams, an endless chase.

With each heartbeat, colors blend,
A canvas drawn, our hearts extend,
In whispered hues of love and grace,
We step into the light's warm face.

Crystal Echoes in the Garden of Wonders

Amidst the blooms of radiant light,
Crystal echoes take their flight,
In gardens lush with dreams aglow,
A world of wonder starts to flow.

Glinting paths of emerald hues,
Whispers carry ancient news,
Secrets held in petals soft,
In every sigh, the spirits loft.

Beneath the stars, the garden wakes,
With every rustle, magic shakes,
Fairy laughter fills the air,
Invoking joy beyond compare.

Reflecting pools of sapphire deep,
Guarding dreams that we may keep,
In silvered light, our hopes align,
As time eternal starts to shine.

In this space where wonders meet,
Life unfolds in moments sweet,
Through crystal echoes, love will flow,
In the garden where dreams grow.

Enchanted Breaths of Starlit Canopy

Beneath the sky of velvet deep,
Where ancient secrets softly sleep,
The whispers of the night shall sing,
Of hidden dreams that night winds bring.

A shimmer drapes the world in white,
As stars twinkle with gentle light,
Their glimmers dance, a twirling show,
In quiet woods where moonbeams flow.

Crickets chirp a lullaby,
While shadows weave and spirits fly,
Each breath a tale, both sweet and rare,
Of journeys taken on a dare.

With every rustle, hope ignites,
In tangled boughs and soft twilight,
The magic swirls through leaves and air,
A tapestry beyond compare.

So close your eyes and feel the breeze,
Let starlit wonders bring you ease,
For in this realm where dreams take flight,
Enchanted breaths weave day and night.

Whispers of Magic in the Moonlit Grove

In shadows draped by silver beams,
The grove awakens, filled with dreams,
Each leaf a story yet untold,
In moonlit whispers, pure and bold.

The owls glide through boughs with grace,
While fireflies twinkle, a dance in place,
Their luminous trails weave through the dark,
Guiding the hearts to hope's bright spark.

A melody forms on the crisp night air,
Of magic rooted deep down there,
With every heartbeat, the forest sighs,
As spellbound nature sings its cries.

Here lost are sorrows, wandering free,
In the embrace of the ancient tree,
Its gnarled bark a keeper close,
Of secrets long held, a silent prose.

Beneath the stars that swirl and gleam,
The moonlight weaves a wondrous dream,
So come, dear friend, let us explore,
The whispers of magic forevermore.

Sparkling Threads of Forgotten Legends

In tales of old where shadows loom,
The echoes of our past still bloom,
Each thread a story lost in time,
A sparkling note, a whispered rhyme.

From dragon's flight to knight's bold quest,
These legends stir within our breast,
Their glories bright, though dimmed by dust,
In woven hearts, we place our trust.

A flicker here, a tale from there,
Of kingdoms lost, of love laid bare,
With every stitch, the fabric grows,
In shimmering hues that time bestows.

So gather 'round, let voices rise,
In folds of lore where magic lies,
For in our dreams, the past shall glow,
Through sparkling threads, the stories flow.

The tapestry awaits our voice,
To weave the past as we rejoice,
For legends live beyond their fate,
In every heart, they resonate.

Veils of Light in the Enchanted Realm

Through veils of light where shadows weave,
An enchanted realm we dare believe,
Each corner glimmers, each path aglow,
A wondrous world, where few may go.

The streams of silver lazily fork,
Where dreams and wishes softly spark,
In gentle ripples, secrets speak,
Of distant realms, both bold and meek.

The flowers bloom in pastel hues,
Each petal whispers ancient views,
They sway and nod as breezes pass,
In this serene, enchanted grass.

With every step, the magic swells,
In every smile, the spirit dwells,
A place where hearts find sweet reprieve,
In warmth of light, we choose to cleave.

So come, dear traveler, lose your way,
In veils of light, let dreams hold sway,
For in this realm of beauty bright,
We find our souls in pure delight.

Vaults of Light Beyond the Stargazer's Reach

In shadows deep where dreams take flight,
The stars convene, a wondrous sight.
Their whispers dance on moonlit waves,
A tapestry where night behaves.

Through cosmic halls the wanderers tread,
With hearts alight, no fears to dread.
Galaxies weave their silent lore,
In whispered tales of yesteryore.

Each twinkling spark a secret shared,
In realms where wishes once declared.
The vaults of light, a canvas wide,
Where hope and wonder gently glide.

Oh, stardust dreams that brightly gleam,
In every child's enchanted dream.
Beyond the reach of earthly sight,
The universe ignites its light.

A journey long, where souls embark,
To chase the ethereal, the spark.
Together bound, through dark they roam,
To find in light, their every home.

Radiance of Melody in a Whispersong

In a garden where the petals sway,
A melody blooms, both soft and gay.
Notes flutter like the wings of bees,
Carried aloft on the gentle breeze.

Whispers weave through the branches high,
Dancing with dreams, they softly sigh.
A harmony that calls the night,
With every breath, the world feels right.

The lilting tunes, like silver rain,
Invoke the joy, the sweet refrain.
Through winding paths of glistening dew,
The serenade breaks forth anew.

A symphony of nature's grace,
In tranquil moments, we embrace.
The whispersong, a timeless art,
That lingers deep within the heart.

As twilight falls and shadows play,
The radiance calls, we must not stray.
For in each note, a magic's spun,
In whispersong, our souls are one.

Shimmering Horizons of the Mythical Sea

Beyond the waves where sunlight gleams,
A world awakens, wrapped in dreams.
The mythical sea, with tales untold,
In shimmering depths, adventures bold.

Waves rise and fall like heartbeat's flow,
In depths where ancient secrets glow.
The ocean's breath, a timeless song,
Where mysteries of the deep belong.

A siren's call beneath the stars,
Calls sailors forth to seek their spar.
In shimmering light, their paths entwined,
By hidden wonders yet to find.

With every crest, new worlds ignite,
In laughter danced by moon's soft light.
The horizon whispers of the bold,
Tales of the brave and the uncontrolled.

So set your sails to the unknown,
And feel the pulse of the sea's own tone.
For in the depths of every wave,
Lie shimmering horizons, wild and brave.

Dreamlit Petals Beneath the Twilight Canopy

In twilight's grasp, the world transforms,
As dreamlit petals take new forms.
A dance of color, soft and bright,
Beneath the canopy of night.

The whispers of the evening breeze,
Play with petals upon the trees.
With each soft touch, a secret told,
Of moments fleeting, dreams unfold.

Silver stars through branches peek,
In this enchanted realm, we seek.
A moonlit glow, a gentle guide,
In twilight's arms, where magic hides.

With every breath, the heart takes wing,
To chase the joy that twilight brings.
Each petal dreams in silent grace,
Beneath the stars, they find their place.

So linger long, where twilight weaves,
A tapestry of hopes and dreams.
In dreamlit petals, let love be found,
Beneath the canopy, all around.

Luminescent Dreams of a Forgotten Fairy

In a glen where shadows sway,
A fairy whispers soft and low,
Her breath the dawn, her wings the day,
With secrets wrapped in silver glow.

Beneath the boughs of ancient trees,
She weaves her tales in moonlit seams,
Each sparkle caught upon the breeze,
A tapestry of timeless dreams.

Lost are the echoes, none recall,
Yet still her laughter shimmers bright,
A melody for one and all,
A spell cast by the fading light.

In twilight's arms, where whispers dwell,
The remnants of her magic gleam,
A story wrapped in every bell,
The heart of night, a softly sighing theme.

So heed the call when shadows play,
For dreams of fairies swirl around,
In journeys bright as break of day,
In glades where lost ones still abound.

Fabled Lights in the Heart of the Night

When stars awaken in the sky,
And blanket all the world below,
The fables of the night draw nigh,
In whispered tales of light and glow.

Beneath the vault of shimmering dreams,
The moonlit paths begin to weave,
In every heart, a secret seems,
A spark of wonder to believe.

The shadows dance with flickering grace,
Encircled by their golden gleam,
In every corner, a warm embrace,
A haven born from starlit dream.

From ancient woods to sapphire seas,
The legends linger ever near,
Each flicker sings, a tender breeze,
In lullabies for those who hear.

So lose yourself in the soft embrace,
Of fabled lights that guide the night,
Within their glow, find your true place,
A constellation, pure delight.

Enigmatic Echoes of the Wooing Wind

Through whispering trees the soft wind calls,
Its secrets wrapped in fragrant air,
It weaves through dreams in quiet thralls,
A haunting song beyond compare.

In every rustle, tales unfold,
Of lovers lost and shadows found,
A symphony of stories told,
In echoes where sweet hopes abound.

Beneath the moon's watchful gaze,
The gathering winds begin to dance,
Through night's embrace, they set ablaze,
A tapestry of fate and chance.

So listen well, when night awakes,
To whispers carried on the breeze,
For every sigh, a promise makes,
In echoes woven through the trees.

With every gust, remember this,
The heart of love is never shy,
For in the wind, a gentle kiss,
Reminds us all of how to fly.

Glowing Comets in a Twilight Dance

When twilight spills across the sky,
And colors blend in soft embrace,
The comets streak, as if to fly,
In glowing trails that light the space.

With every tail, a wish is spun,
A story etched in dreams anew,
The night alive, a dance begun,
With every spark, a heart's adieu.

They paint the heavens, fleeting beams,
In whispers of the universe,
Each comet holds the light of dreams,
A cosmic serenade, diverse.

As shadows yield to starry flame,
The twilight spins its magic bright,
A sonnet sung, and yet the same,
We are but sparks beneath the night.

So chase the glow as daylight fades,
And let your spirit soar and prance,
For in the dance of twilight shades,
We find our place in time's romance.

Misty Glimmers in Ethereal Light

In the hush of twilight's grace,
Misty glimmers softly trace,
Whispers from a fading day,
In the night they dance and sway.

Faintly glows the silver mist,
Where ancient tales will twist,
Stars peek through the gentle veil,
Each one holding a secret tale.

A river flows of dreams untold,
Carrying wishes, brave and bold,
As shadows weave their mystic art,
In the echoes, love will start.

Beneath the boughs of emerald trees,
The world whispers with the breeze,
In the stillness, hearts ignite,
Bathed in soft, ethereal light.

With each sigh, a longing grows,
In the dark, a soft light glows,
Misty glimmers in the night,
Awake the dreams, guide their flight.

Celestial Whispers of Dreaming Stars

In the depths of night so deep,
Celestial whispers softly seep,
Through the veil of endless skies,
Where the slumbering magic lies.

Stars like jewels, vast and bright,
Glitter softly, pure delight,
Every twinkle tells a tale,
Of wondrous dreams that never pale.

Among the clouds, a symphony,
Echoes sweetly, wild and free,
Each note weaves a silken thread,
Binding lives that dream in bed.

Space embraces, warm and wide,
Welcoming the hopes inside,
With each pulse, the cosmos calls,
In its arms, no one falls.

Awake, dear heart, the dawn will break,
With every wish that we do make,
Celestial whispers guide our way,
In the light of a brand new day.

Luminescent Tendrils of Fabled Dawn

As night gives way to morning light,
Luminescent tendrils take flight,
Dancing gently on the breeze,
Awakening the sleeping trees.

Golden rays stretch far and wide,
Awash in colors, joy and pride,
Painting skies with vibrant hues,
A canvas rich that nature chews.

Softly whispers the gentle sun,
To every heart, its warmth begun,
In the hush of freshened air,
Hope resides, enchantments rare.

With dawn's embrace, the shadows flee,
Every moment wild and free,
Tendrils rise and intertwine,
In the blush of day divine.

The world awakens, bright and clear,
Each heartbeat sings, the world draws near,
In this orb of painted dawn,
Fabled dreams are reborn.

Sparkling Echoes in the Enchanted Glade

In the heart of the ancient wood,
Sparkling echoes rise and flood,
Where magic lingers in the air,
In the glade that holds such care.

Dreams take flight on wings of glee,
Whispers float from tree to tree,
Every leaf, a story spun,
In the twilight, all is one.

Moonlight bathes the world in song,
In the glade, where hearts belong,
Casting spells in silver beams,
Awakening the lost dreams.

Footsteps dance on mossy ground,
To the rhythm of the sound,
Nature hums a lullaby,
As stars begin to light the sky.

In this haven, love ignites,
With every breath, the magic bites,
Sparkling echoes, soft and true,
In the glade, where dreams renew.